C Fox

TREAT FOR YOU

# FINDING THE RIGHT RETREAT FOR YOU

GILLEAN RUSSELL

Series editor Jeanne Hinton

Copyright © 1994 Hunt & Thorpe
Text © Gillean Russell
Cover Illustration © Len Munnik

ISBN 1 85608 118 4

In Australia this book is published by:
Hunt & Thorpe Australia Pty Ltd.
9 Euston Street, Rydalmere NSW 2116

A CIP catalogue record for this book is available from the British Library

Manufactured in the United Kingdom

# CONTENTS

# ■ INTRODUCTION

In the last 20 years or so holidays have developed in all kinds of ways. Never mind the package deal, there are all sorts of DIY holidays advertised in the UK and all over the Continent. You can sign up for summer schools or spend a week looking at National Trust properties, you can learn to paint or go pony trekking on Dartmoor, you can spend time learning new watersports or go cycling round East Anglia. All manner of holidays for people with every kind of interest can now be arranged.

This booklet is about a different sort of holiday, it is about retreats, which you could call 'holidays with God'. One of the reasons that retreats have become so popular in recent years is that they now cater for people of very different spiritual backgrounds and personality types. The needs of many more people are now being met by the different retreat styles.

Thirty years ago retreats were thought to be only for the 'spiritual elite', nowadays they make sense to many people on the fringes of the church. The hunger for meaning in life is very strong and retreats provide space for reflection and the processing of the events of our lives, something we have lost in an age of fast travel and fast food – jet lag and indigestion!

Many people today are struck by the idea of a retreat, the chance to 'get away from it all'. Just as our bodies and minds need a break from routine, so our spiritual side, the reflective part of us, needs time for recreation and nourishment. There are all sorts of ways of finding such refreshment.

This is a book about noticing and keeping account of God's gifts to us and it is about one setting in which this process can be begun and renewed.

The first section may answer some of the questions that could be running through your mind about retreats. The second section gives an account of what to expect from the different styles of retreat. It is written in the belief that love is attractive and it follows that the Creator God who loves each one of us is a God who attracts us and draws us to himself. So if you are attracted to the idea of making a retreat, of spending time with God, you are responding to love's invitation, which is what you were created for.

Gillean Russell
April 1994

# ■ I
# LOITERING WITH INTENT

WHEN A dedicated burglar plans a robbery he goes about it in a very determined way. He assesses the value of the goods to him and has in mind a use or an outlet for them. He locates the prize as precisely as he can and then he will watch and wait, noting the comings and goings of those who live or work in the vicinity, their relationships and habits. All his efforts are concentrated on the job of acquiring the goods.

This is supposed to be a book about spending time with God, not appraising the work of criminals, but when it comes to getting something we really want, then the discerning thief has something to show us.

What is really striking is the thief's single-mindedness, and how his *wanting* gives him the energy to plan and to achieve. The more seriously we want something the more single-minded we become and the more likely we are to get what we seek, because of the new energy available to us.

We have talked about the robber and his ill-gotten gains, but what about wanting good things, things to which we are entitled? What about the longing of the lover for the beloved? What about the human desire to become fully a person, what about the longing for meaning in life – for God? Sometimes we need to ask ourselves if we go about our Christian journey with anything like the energy that we give to the pursuit of career status, finding a partner, a new home, a new car – or whatever our consuming passion may be.

## ■ A PERSONAL JOURNEY

You may feel that you would like to give more time and energy to deepening your relationship with God, so that it flows out into your daily life and into your relationships.

House groups and bible studies help us to attend to God at the head level, but how do we attend to him (or her) at the heart level? How do we get to know him as distinct from knowing about him? Part of this is a journey we make in common with other Christians, praying with the church in liturgical worship or praying in groups where spontaneous prayer is practised. But there is also a personal journey to be made. It is with this part of the journey that we are concerned here.

As Christians, as living beings, we accept ourselves as creatures of the Creator. This makes us part of the living world of plants and animals, but different from them in what we believe (or claim to believe) that we are made in the likeness of God. What a claim!

What enormous possibilities this opens up. We may feel that the likeness of God is very well concealed in us and by us, but there is the potential for its gradual release or realisation as we come to know God. The more we come to know him the more we become free to be the creatures he made us to be, and we glimpse a quality of life that the bible calls abundant, or eternal life. It is in becoming what God made us to be that we are most truly ourselves and most truly free. St Irenaeus said that 'the glory of God is a human being fully alive!'

The call to prayer is the call to become fully alive.

## ■ A DEEPER EXPLORATION

Prayer is about a relationship with God and, like most relationships, it operates on different levels. Sometimes it is about remembering others who are in need, sometimes it is rejoicing in a relationship or exulting in the beauty of nature. Often it is wrestling with a situation from which God seems to have withdrawn, like famine or civil war, or some more personal disaster.

We may turn to God when we are ill or bereaved. Sometimes we seek comfort, sometimes we pound him with painful and heartfelt questions, and because an answer (in the way we expect) does not come we conclude that either we have not prayed 'properly', or that God isn't listening. Do not be put off but allow yourself to be led on into a deeper exploration of what prayer is about. Stay with the longing, the pain perhaps. Stay with your need to find meaning in the situation, for it is in our emptiness that there is room for God.

We are more likely to find God when we are aware of something lacking, or of a desparate 'wanting'. There are times in life when we give up 'everything' to get through an exam or to win or woo a partner, so we know how it feels to be single-minded. The wholehearted *wanting* galvanises us into action. It is dynamic! The same is true of spiritual longing, it provides fuel for the search.

When the wanting becomes sufficiently strong we will leave no stone unturned in order to find the object of our search. We let go of some of our more superficial longings in order to devote ourselves to the deeper one. Somewhere, underneath the turbulence of everyday relating and working and the short bursts of single-mindedness, there is a deeper thread that we occasionally touch – the thread of *meaning*.

The spiritual search is a search for meaning in our lives.

**For you to do:** What has led you to read this booklet? Are you aware of something lacking in your life ... or a search for ... what?

Spend some time thinking about this, and then write a few words or draw a picture that captures a little of what you are feeling and thinking.

There will be similar exercises throughout the booklet, and it will help to have a notebook or journal in which you can write or draw as you work through these exercises.

## ■ WHY ARE YOU?

Among our first goals in early adult life are a career, a partner, marriage, a family – all things which go towards the necessary establishment of identity. This is the important stage of 'ego development'. That is the development of the conscious self which relates, and must relate, to the outer world. We are not at ease in the outer world if we neglect this stage of development. It is about who we are and what we stand for. Christians often get a bit worried about ego development because they think it sounds 'selfish' or 'worldly', but it is as essential to our psychic life as the fully developed bones in our body are to our physical maturity. Usually it is only when we have done most of the work on our identity, and have established our place in society, that we begin to look for meaning. What we may notice then is that, all of a sudden, there is no dynamo, no driving force to direct our lives. We stop asking 'where am I going?' and ask, instead, 'why am I here?'

Many become aware of this kind of spiritual hunger in their middle years as they enter a period of some kind of bereavement; a loss of status as a parent when the children leave home, or a loss of challenge at work because all the battles have been fought. However good the partnerships and friendships, however satisfying the success at work, there rises the nagging question – 'what's it all *for*?'

This is a question that many find confronting them when they take time to reflect upon their lives. Stripped of the various roles which, we believed, made us meaningful we may feel exposed and uncomfortable. Some people will cope by trying to ignore the questions, others will make a compromise and try to find new roles to boost their confidence. But we do well if we try to attend to our discomfiture and discover where it is leading us. It can be a lonely time and a challenging one, but if you have reached the pitch when you have to attend to it, a retreat may be a considerable help.

## ■ TRAVELLING TOWARDS THE MORE

If you find yourself resonating with some of these thoughts you may be in touch with your hunger, your spiritual hunger. You are becoming aware of a need. You are beginning to search for new answers.

Sometimes people make their search in inappropriate places, underestimating the depth of the search's origin. Is the longing really for a new partner, a new job or anything *out there*, or is it something about the inner life?

The search for change and development in the middle years is a very natural one, and a day or two away to get a perspective on it in a retreat setting can help. It may help us avoid the frustration of searching in the wrong place, for something that is much deeper, the search for meaning, for integration, for God *within us*.

I remember when I was about six years old my brother got scarlet fever, which was treated as a serious illness at that time. He was sent to an isolation hospital and I was sure that he would die. I remember praying ardently for his recovery. For my brother the episode is long forgotten, but for me it was the time that I first turned to God with a need and it was the beginning of the most important journey of my life, although I did not realise it at the time.

We each start our journey from a different experience, but it is likely that it will be an awareness of incompleteness or powerlessness which will start us groping towards God. I don't just mean that it happens when some inadequacy is discovered or when we can't cope with a situation. It may be an overwhelming experience of something beyond ourselves, the magnificence of a sunset or the generosity of a friend that starts the search – not things that in any way belittle us but things that show us how much *more* there is and increase our longing to travel towards the more.

God is a God who attracts: 'Thou hast made us for thyself and our hearts are restless till they rest in Thee.' (St Augustine). We need to lose the image that so many people carry (often unconsciously) of God as a tyrant, waiting to come down on us as soon as we put a foot wrong. God is the source of love who longs for us to be connected with him at every level of our being, so that we may live in tune with his design.

**For you to do:** What goals have you achieved in your life to date? What has motivated you and given you energy?

# ■ 2
# WHO IS PURSUING YOU?

MOST OF US have an idea that we should 'say prayers' every day but even the most committed Christian finds this an effort at times. Some find help in praying with others, and from doing so learn much about the need for diversity of approach. People differ and their style of prayer differs.

What we come to learn, in time, is that it is God who is pursuing *us*! Our particular personality will affect our approach to a relationship with God, just as it affects our relationships with other people. One way of praying is no better than any other and we have much to learn from each other. In the end, however, God will develop his relationship with each of us in a unique way.

It is often helpful to have someone to talk to about our experience in prayer, someone who can help us to reflect on the way God deals with us. Someone who can help us see the context of our life in God and all its facets.

Some people seek help from the clergy. It is a mistake to assume that they are too busy, for this is one of the most important things for which they are ordained and many of them would rather spend time helping a person to pray than doing some of their more mundane tasks. Sometimes another member of the church may be approached to give help. If the person you ask can't help, they may be able to suggest someone who can.

Many Christians have someone they see on a regular basis for spiritual guidance. The spiritual director/guide, or soul friend, is someone who walks alongside you in your journey of prayer; she or he will help you to reflect on your experience and find a way of prayer that is helpful to you. This may be an informal arrangement with a friend or a more formal one with someone outside your immediate circle. It is important that the person you choose to talk to is someone you feel at ease with, so that you can be yourself and talk from your heart.

What we often lack is the time and the opportunity to reflect on our life experience and what it has to show us. Our life experience *is* experience of God, for he is the creator at work making us into the people he would have us be. How does he shape us? How does he show us what we need to see? What is his love like and how does he draw us to himself? You may search many learned books for the answers, but the person who really helps you is the one who listens to your experience and helps you to see how God has been in it.

## ■ A LIVING RELATIONSHIP

Prayer is not a textbook subject, but a living relationship, so the only way we really learn to pray is by praying. Like study, we learn best if we set time aside and put our learning into practice as we go along. Even if they live alone, most people find it a hard discipline to give time to prayer at home. How to find time in the course of a day which is often programmed from the moment you wake until the moment your head hits the pillow at night is a very real difficulty.

The ideal is, of course, to 'pray without ceasing' or to 'find God in all things' so that you can know your whole day to be prayer, a day lived out consciously in the presence of God. Not many of us can do that without a lot of practice on the nursery slopes at first!

If your time at home seems too full, or there are always people around, it can be helpful to find a church that is open during the day and to spend a few minutes in the quiet there. It is sad that many churches are closed during the day, but if you do find one open it is there so that people may use it for prayer, so feel free to take advantage of it.

Nevertheless the time may come when you feel you need a longer time to consider your relationship to God, and more importantly, God's relationship with you. This may have led you to want to discover more about retreats.

**For you to do:** Who are the people who have helped you on your way? Who has listened to you? Have you had an experience of God or of 'something other'? Perhaps God is a bit like the people you have just thought of?

This is one of the ways in which God can make himself known to us.

# ■ 3
# RELAX AND LISTEN

A RETREAT IS a time consciously set aside for God. It is a period of time, usually a day or a weekend, sometimes longer. It may take one of several forms, and there will be more information about the different kinds of retreat given later on. It is a time for exploration, a time when you can discover and practise different ways of listening to God and responding to him, time to become more aware of the way God is to be found in creation and in your life experience. When you make a retreat you are free from all domestic or work responsibilities and you are in a quiet place so that all the channels of communication are open and ready.

Some retreat houses are set in beautiful countryside 'away from it all' and others may be found in a city environment. Many of them offer a day programme for exploring prayer – quiet days or drop-in days – and for many people this is a good way to start. Such a day will be loosely structured with two or three talks, often a service of Holy Communion, and time for quiet prayer and reflection. The talks are designed to lead people to prayer, and the leader is also usually available to talk with those who ask for particular help. The programme normally includes meals/refreshments. Good food is very important on such a day!

## ■ PREPARING TO PRAY

If you can't locate a planned quiet day many retreat houses offer accommodation for the day for anyone wishing to come on their own. There is often someone available to talk to who can offer suggestions about using the day. Some church groups arrange quiet days in their own setting and, if there are a number of people in a church wanting to explore prayer, it is a good idea to invite someone to come and lead one in your church or in someone's house. It needs to be somewhere reasonably quiet where interruptions are as few as possible – unplug the telephone and send the children out for the day! Enough room is required for people to spread out and find their own space to be quiet.

A leader for the day will make some specific suggestions which you will be invited to follow. Perhaps it is helpful to say that prayer is one of God's greatest gifts and we can only prepare to receive it, so these suggestions are likely not so much to tell you *how* to pray, but how to *prepare* yourself to pray, and we can all do that. It is said that Archbishop Michael Ramsay was once asked how long he spent in prayer and his reply was that he spent 29 minutes preparing to pray and one minute praying!

It is important to remember that God is the God of love and that he longs to communicate with us. We too easily complain that God doesn't talk to *us*, when the fact is that we have not learned to listen to him. We must spend time learning to listen before we dare to say that prayer is not for us. Start by allowing yourself to know that God loves you and that he wants you to know that. That particular 'penny' drops ever deeper as our life of prayer grows, God cannot tell us enough how much he loves us and our true freedom stems from the heart knowledge of that fact.

Preparation for prayer is about disposing ourselves, loitering with intent again, to hear and see what he wishes to show us. We put ourselves in God's way. We do this in a more obvious and significant way when we actually go and spend a day or a weekend with him. We mean business!

We prepare ourselves for prayer as we prepare ourselves to listen to someone who loves and respects us. To do this it is important to be in a place where you will not be interrupted and where the distractions are as few as possible. A retreat house, which is especially set aside for people who want to be quiet to attend to God, is an ideal setting. To be looked after with homely simplicity, in a warm and accepting atmosphere, positively draws you into the time of retreat. You set aside the concerns of everyday living and enjoy being looked after. You begin to relate to a nurturing God who cares for you in every way. Those who look after the guests (or retreatants) in the house will welcome you and make sure that you have what you need but they will not fuss you. You will soon begin to feel relaxed, and perhaps a little excited ....

**For you to do:** Go out for a walk and spend about five minutes walking slowly and looking at all there is to see. Notice the colours and textures around. Then spend five minutes listening. First to the loud and obvious sounds you can hear and then to the more distant and fainter sounds – the birds, the distant hum of traffic. Try touching things – the barks of different trees, the roughness of a wall, the softness of moss.

Don't be in a hurry to move on, and be aware how much more is going on than we usually notice.

# 4

# RETREAT AND GAIN PERSPECTIVE

A RETREAT, on a very practical level, moves us from our usual responsibilities and relationships and sets them in a different perspective. Given the space, we can become objective observers of our feelings, confusion, ideals and aspirations, relationships and, of course, any particular problems or griefs that trouble us.

With space to listen we ask God to show us what he would have us see – what needs appraisal or adjustment, what needs nurturing or pruning. There may be much more to look at than you could possibly attempt in the space of a short weekend, in which case it is a good idea to prioritise before you go, or during the first few hours of the retreat, so that you don't spend the whole weekend deciding what you want to focus on.

A retreat gives us an opportunity to attend to our relationship with ourselves, with others and with God. Perhaps you think it strange to put God last there – surely a retreat is a time for putting God first? What we need to remember is that we can really only start on this adventure from where we are. We start with what is real in our lives now – the feelings and aspirations that we have, the relationships we arc in and the images of God that we hold.

No one can tell us what God is like and we have to make do with images and metaphors and partial truths. Most of our images are built unconsciously on our limited experience and if we think of God, for instance, as Father, it is almost impossible not to identify him with the father we know, or the father figure we know. Many people are crippled by the image of a vengeful and angry father, a weak and absent one, or an unknown and deserting father. Perhaps with time to reflect they will find it easier to relate to God who reveals himself in Jesus as a brother. A new relationship may then begin to grow.

Julian of Norwich, an English 14th-century mystic, spoke of seeing God as 'our mother' and this is an image that we are meeting again in our own time. The image of a nurturing, close and restoring mother, a mother who looks with loving regard on her growing child and is there to affirm every sign of new growth, is a wonderful foundation for our image of God. Mother, father, spouse – all intimate relationships

– are but a few of the ways in which we may apprehend God.

Thinking of God as 'she', even talking about 'her', may enable a new and different relationship. For simplicity's sake I have talked about 'him' in this booklet but it isn't always the way I think about her.

Remember that God's greatest gift to us is the gift of ourselves through which we may grow to know him and to love him. The images we have of ourselves (often as unloveable) are just as hard to come to terms with.

## ■ EXPERIENCE OF BEING PAMPERED

My guess is that the reason why many more people are finding retreats helpful is that new styles have developed which enable people to find God in their own experience. All of us are likely to have had a 'religious experience' at some time in our lives, but we may not have recognised it as such.

God has different ways of making himself known to us, for some it will be the dawning of some truth, for others an experience of the senses – the beauty of nature, a breathtaking view from a mountain top. One person may have 'hunches' about God's presence, and another will find God through a deep relationship and feelings. At different times in our lives we may be touched at all these levels, but some will give us cause to catch our breath (an 'ah' experience) more than others. During a retreat our sole purpose is to spend time with God, to become more aware of his presence in our lives and in the lives of others, to learn more about the way he communicates with us and what our response to this might be in daily life and work.

Everything on a retreat is geared to help *you* to feel special. Although you may be with others, your individual needs will be attended to. The quiet in the house is comfortable and purposeful and you will find the staff friendly and outgoing. The quiet is a comfortable quiet which invites you to bask in God's love and acceptance. It is a wonderful experience of being spoilt and pampered.

We flourish if we grow up knowing ourselves loved. The story of God's love affair with us begins in a garden. If we persevere with retreats we shall find that God moves us on and our journey with him will take us to the wilderness too. The process of being created is a lifelong and exacting one.

**For you to do:** What would you say if someone asked you to describe yourself in two sentences, leaving out your single/marital/ parental status or your occupation. What do you most like about being you?

# ■ 5

# WHAT TO EXPECT

As WELL AS feeling excited it is very natural to feel a bit apprehensive about the unknown and the unfamiliar.

Most retreats start near a meal time and there will be a chance to talk to the others, some of whom may have made a retreat before and will probably tell you what an important place a regular retreat has in their lives for exploration and stocktaking. Others in the group may also be there for the first time.

Occasionally there are retreats run especially with first timers in mind, such retreats may be called 'an adventure into silence' and suggestions will be given as to how to adjust and use such a period of silence. Afterwards you are likely to be surprised how easy it was and also surprised how much you noticed about others in the silence, for most retreats are usually silent after the opening talk, or address, the silence is usually broken at the last meal. Nervousness about the unfamiliar silence sometimes makes people 'get the giggles' but it is soon overcome as you get engaged in what the retreat is about!

The size of a group attending a retreat may vary but it is usually between about 10 and 30 people, nearly always a group of mixed ages and sexes, though the middle-aged (30-65!) tend to predominate. Usually you will have a room to yourself and there are often one or two sitting rooms in the retreat house, and also a garden. The timetable will include the times of the addresses (usually two or three each day) which last for 15 or 20 minutes. They may be given in the chapel or in a sitting room.

Nothing is obligatory on a retreat. You may not necessarily find the addresses helpful (the leader cannot always give addresses that speak to everyone!) but you should give them a fair trial and perhaps go and talk with her or him about any difficulties you are experiencing.

A retreat is also a chance to get some extra sleep. For this reason the day may start late and finish early and afternoons are usually free for sleeping or walking. Most people find the experience so relaxing they sleep well both in the afternoon and at night.

Anyone can go on a retreat but those who are searching for something, whether they only sense it as a 'spiritual dimension', or a search for meaning, or more clearly for God, will profit most.

It would be wise to add here that retreats are

not the answer to everyone's problems. It is unwise to go to a retreat if you are badly depressed because the depression may be heightened by the unfamiliarity of the place and the silence. This may be a time to get some more sustained help from your doctor or a counsellor. You may choose to go on a retreat later when you are feeling more at ease with yourself.

If you are battling with some problem in your life which tends to take over when you are still, a retreat again may not be the answer. You may find yourself swamped by the problem. We say we must 'get away from it all' and doing that in the physical sense may land us right in the thick of it in the psychological sense, and we may not be able to attend to God in the way that we had hoped. If you are in any doubt, sound it out with someone who knows you well.

Some aspects of a retreat may be a bit daunting until their reason is understood. There will be the lack of the usual distractions, radios and TV, chatter, and (for some of us) food or drink in excess.

Have you ever noticed how good a piece of bread can taste when there is nothing else to eat and you are hungry? How often are you really hungry? How can we know what it is like to starve in Somalia if there is always a super-abundance of food in our own larders? With the many refined and exotic foods available to us we may find it difficult to choose between them. This masks our total dependence on God. We are confident of the arrival of the next meal and we know nothing of the experience of people who are lucky if they get food at all and may never have the chance of choosing what it is. At last, during a retreat, there is time to stop and take life in slow motion, valuing and savouring all the things we normally take for granted. Enjoying the simple, good food with which we are provided without being choosy could be used to help us to a renewed sense of dependency on God who provides enough for all.

Most of us keep busy if we don't like our own company and busyness becomes a prop which protects us from anxiety or other uncomfortable feelings. At first we chafe at this deprivation until we come to see where it points. Keeping silence expresses our desire to listen to God. You will be aware of other, and often deeper ways of communication when you enter a period of silence. Our lives are so busy with sophisticated and superficial things that we have largely lost touch with the basics of life, our dependence on the rain and the sun, the simplicity of a flower or a tree and the wealth of things to be learned from contemplating them.

We natter on at one another, but when we have to communicate without words we become much more attentive to each other and begin to notice a whole new range of things about other people.

It may begin to sound as though a retreat is a panacea for all ills, but it is *not* a running away from our problems. It *is* a running to God with our lives and asking him to do some stocktaking with us so that we may return to our daily lives knowing more of where our strength lies and who it is who loves us.

It can take a long time, first to believe, and then to know that we are loved. This is a process that may begin within a retreat, but will need to be followed through in daily life after the retreat.

A retreat is not about learning to live a separate 'spiritual' life which sets us apart from everyday life. Jesus' time of retreat in the wilderness was a time when he faced and identified the temptations which would beset him subtly throughout his ministry. It was a time of facing reality and learning to cope with it. Only after that could his real ministry begin.

**For you to do:** Can you think of a period of time (short or long) when you enjoyed being alone? Where were you and what was special about that time? Describe it in a few sentences.

# 6

# WHAT KIND OF RETREAT SHALL I CHOOSE?

There are about 200 retreat houses in the UK so there is a wealth to choose from. You can find the details of where they are and when the retreats are held in the journal of the National Retreat Association, *The Vision*. This can be obtained by post from NRA, Liddon House, 24 South Audley Street, London W1Y 5DL. Tel 071-493 3534. You can also get help from them, or from the individual retreat houses, if you want more information or guidance in your choice.

Retreats fall into six main groups:

- Conducted retreats
- Individually guided retreats
- Theme retreats
- Private retreats
- Various kinds of awareness workshops
- Retreats in daily life

## ■ A SHORT CONDUCTED RETREAT

I have put this kind of retreat in first because it is the kind that most people know about and it is a good place to start.

It is not always easy to 'drop in' to silence and some structure can be helpful for 'beginners'. At a conducted retreat there is a timetable of services, talks or addresses, meals and free time for walking or resting. Some leaders discourage reading but retreat house libraries or bookstalls can be hard for bookworms to resist. The best kind of reading during a retreat is the bible, or perhaps a good biography.

Anne decided that she would like to start with such a retreat – either for a day or a weekend. She found out about her local retreat house, a beautiful old property in the middle of the country, only 15 miles from the city where she lived, and booked herself a place on a weekend retreat. She was lucky – the leader was quite well known and there was only one place left.

Anne had talked to people who had already been to the retreat house and their comments encouraged her. She found herself getting quite excited as the weekend approached. She had not told anyone at work what she was doing because she was afraid they would think it strange.

She found her way there after work one Friday night in the spring. She was met by a friendly woman who showed her to a room at the top of the house where she had a view of the extensive garden. At supper she met up with about 25 others who had also come for the retreat. Some had been to retreats before and were very reassuring. One of them said that her annual retreat was as important as her annual holiday.

After supper the group gathered in the sitting room and were told a little about the work of a retreat house and how, in recent years, more and more people were coming away for retreats. The leader then suggested that they should move to the chapel and at that point the retreat would begin. They would keep silence until lunchtime on Sunday.

He started off by talking about the collection of different quartz formations he had brought with him, some crystal, some amethyst, which he held up for them to see. They were, he said, millions of years old. They had been collected in the Hebrides somewhere near Fingal's cave, and they had been there through all the years of history that we know about and long, long before.

Anne's imagination began to work as the leader spoke. God *was* even before those stones were formed. Her picture of God began to expand as she thought about it. Later, when the talk was over she had a closer look at the stones and realised that she was handling thousands of years of history. She was in touch with something really ancient, beautiful and wonderfully made. She was handling some part of God's creation which had survived storms, battles, droughts and seasons way back beyond her imagining. The wonder and the immensity of God became very real as she thought about all this in the time of silence that followed the talk. After the silence they took part in the night service of compline.

Anne went straight to her room afterwards, pleased to have an early night. She wanted to go on thinking about what had been said that she had found so mind-boggling, and she decided not to read before going to sleep.

She woke early and decided to get up and explore the garden, where she watched a robin for a full five minutes as he pulled a worm out of the ground. She looked at the dew on a cobweb and wondered at the ingenuity of the spider. She listened to the singing of a bird and saw the tracks of a rabbit in the dew. These were all things she could do at home, but somehow she never did. Life was always too busy.

At breakfast she felt awkward in the silence until she began to notice how people were looking after each other. She noticed that someone always passed her what she needed, and she didn't have to ask. During the morning there was another talk which picked up a theme from the night before. The leader suggested that they should spend half an hour walking round the garden, noticing things, smelling, tasting, listening and looking at the wonders of creation. This linked up with Anne's earlier experience and she enjoyed continuing her appreciation of God's presence in nature. At lunch there was music playing in the dining room which was a helpful backcloth to her thoughts and eased any remaining awkwardness about not talking. She was surprised how tired she felt and after lunch she had a sleep.

There was another talk after tea and another 'exercise' to apply what had been said to her own experience. After supper there was a meditation led by the conductor which introduced her to the possibilities of pondering on all that had been said and had happened during the day. She realised she had questions she wanted to ask and she began to feel the need to talk to someone, so she arranged a time to see the conductor the next morning.

He helped her to make more sense of her thoughts and feelings, mostly by listening to her and helping her to see the patterns behind what felt like a jumble of thoughts and words. She had worried a bit lest he should think she was wasting his time, but was very glad that she had taken the chance to talk with him. She had never really talked to anyone before about God.

There was a communion service before lunch. It was good to sing after resting her voice for so long and she enjoyed the service, taken slowly and thoughtfully. The last talk was given after lunch and there was time to meet up with the other retreatants before leaving for home at teatime. She was surprised to find that she didn't much want to talk to anyone. Many things were in her mind and she wanted a little longer to sort them through before she went home. So she took a country road and went home slowly and made a few notes about the experience.

She felt very good, calm and sustained by her weekend and found herself looking forward to going in to work the next day and telling her friends about it all. She also wondered what difference the retreat might make in her everyday life. There was so much she wanted to test out.

## ■ A LONGER INDIVIDUALLY GUIDED RETREAT

We are now going to leap to the other end of the retreat spectrum and follow the experience of someone who made one of the longer retreats, the 30-day retreat on the Spiritual Exercises of St Ignatius. I have chosen to do this because nowadays most other forms of retreat have their roots in this method even though it may not be recognisable! Few may make the full 30-day retreat but the process has been adapted, simplified and shortened to suit a wide variety of people. The original inspiration for providing people with this method of deepening their faith and discipleship comes from St Ignatius of Loyola who lived in 16th-century Spain.

Three days in silence may sound a long time, but 30 days…! You may think that only monks and nuns would even consider it, but you would be surprised how many ordinary people spend a month in one of the five or six retreat centres where this kind of retreat is available.

Mark was one of them. He was in his 40s and felt that his job no longer gave him satisfaction. He was happily married and it seemed irresponsible to be thinking of changing his job when he had family commitments and no real reason to change, apart from a niggle – was he called to full time ministry or to serve God as a missionary? The niggle would not go away, but yet Mark could not accept that such a drastic change was a real possibility for him.

Mark had been brought up as a Christian –

that he was a Christian was a fact he had never questioned. Faith had come easily to him, but he felt it did not go as deep as it should. He prayed when he remembered, but had found God mostly in his contact with people at work and at church. He felt that he needed thinking time. He needed to get away from the job and from home to get a perspective on the situation. He wished he could find a way to pray about his niggle, but did not know how to go about this satisfactorily.

Sue, his wife, encouraged him when he told her that he was thinking of going away for an individually guided retreat. She was not so keen that he should be away for a month, but she was bothered by his restlessness and felt he had to do something about it.

The retreat centre was some way away and as he travelled Mark wondered how he was going to cope with the month ahead. Could he really fulfil what he had decided to do – the full Spiritual Exercises of St Ignatius. This is a scheme of prayer outlined by St Ignatius in the 16th Century. He was the founder of the Society of Jesus, a group of men who were inspired by his teaching and example and dedicated their lives to apostolic work. The Jesuits today are noted for their involvement in the world, their concern for justice and peace and for their political involvement alongside the weak and the poor.

Intellectually, too, they are often found to be very advanced and radical in their thinking. Their way of life is inspired by this Ignatian way of prayer. It helps them to follow Christ closely, to reflect constantly on the Lord's presence in their experience, in their relationships and in the world around them. Ignatius held out to them the ideal of 'finding God in all things'. They do this by being 'contemplatives in action'.

The exercises were designed to be 'made' or taken in a retreat setting, mostly in silence, and under the direction and guidance of someone familiar with the path. Normally people would make this kind of retreat once in a lifetime and very often with the hope of finding God's will over some really important decision.

Mark felt that this would be a very thorough way of finding out where his life was meant to go, and he entered the retreat house with high hopes.

His director, or guide, to his surprise, was not a monk or a nun, but a lay woman. She seemed to have a good understanding of his situation and his desire to find and do God's will. For a few days he rested, rather wishing that he had not come to the retreat so tired. He saw his director every day and gradually started the exercises. He found that he was praying for five hours a day. It surprised him that he could do this! He was given material to use in these prayer times, and each day he talked with his guide about what happened.

He was introduced to different ways of praying, some he found more helpful than others. He kept a journal and in looking back over his life became aware in a new way of God's love and goodness, and of his purpose for every person. Mark had sometimes said that if he had lived in the time of Jesus he would have had no problem following him, but that somehow the 'churchianity' that had overlaid the years since those times had obscured the Christian path for him. Now he felt as though he, too, had walked the Galilean hills with his Lord.

At the end of the retreat his expectations had changed. He left the house with a new sense of God's love for him, God's trust in him and a desire to serve him in all that he did. Many of his old ideas about God had been turned inside out and he had come out the stronger for it. He had had an experience which he could only describe as one of conversion. God had turned him to himself. He still had to face the decision about his job, but he felt less anxious about that, it was no longer a real issue for him.

Some months later the opportunity to move into an area of voluntary political work occurred. Mark had always fought shy of such involvement before. He did not, in the end, change his job but became very involved with working for the rights of a minority group in his neighbourhood. Mark realised how glad he was to have been shown another way of living a committed Christian life. A change of job had never quite made sense after all his training and experience, but finding his voice in the cause of an oppressed group brought him new strength and new wisdom and he recognised this as an answer to his prayer.

## ■ A SHORTER INDIVIDUALLY GUIDED RETREAT

Mark's wife, Sue, was delighted when Mark came back from his retreat with lots to tell her, but not the news she dreaded – that they were to pull up their roots and start a new life somewhere else. She noticed that he seemed to have more confidence and was certainly more at peace with himself. There was something else about him that she could not quite name, perhaps *joy* was the word. She was deeply impressed and decided that she would make a similar retreat – not that she could afford the time or the money to make the 30 days.

Mark told her that there was a shorter version based on the kind of retreat that he had made.

Sue found another retreat centre not far from London where she booked in for an eight-day, individually guided retreat the following autumn. She stayed in a Roman Catholic convent in the stockbroker belt and enjoyed the beautiful garden and the walks in the woods close by. She met with Sister Marie each day and told her about her own spiritual journey. One of the things she did was to spend some time reflecting on her life to see how God had been at work there. Sr Marie asked what experiences, which people, had given her a notion of who God is, and she began to piece together her 'faith history' and noticed the stepping stones which had brought her to her present belief and religious practice.

Sue always thought that other people had 'religious experiences' but that God didn't talk to her in a direct or recognisable way. By the time she had spent a day pondering on her faith story she realised that this was not true. God had certainly been active in her life only she had never had time to reflect and see just how much experience she had had. This enabled her to stop worrying that she was not as good as others. She felt affirmed by God when she was helped to see how much he loved her. She spent the week praying with passages of scripture that Sr Marie chose for her each day, which made God's love for her very real and very personal.

During her free time Sue worked with clay and found that using her hands in this way gave her another slant on prayer. She also went for some long walks and found that the thoughts begun in her prayer time developed as she walked and took in the landscapes around her. The lakes and the trees spoke to her of God's love. Although she had nothing to do but to meet Sr Marie each day and to keep to her prayer times (she had decided to pray for an hour four times a day), she found that she did not have a lot of time to spare. The convent had a pleasant chapel which was warm and carpeted and sometimes she prayed there. Sometimes she prayed in a smaller prayer room, which had some beautful things in it – a piece of weathered wood, an icon, an old earthenware pitcher, a bowl of water, a lighted candle. There was also a cross made from an old tree. She found these symbols very helpful.

One way of prayer which was suggested to her was that she should imagine herself within a gospel scene and listen and watch as the Lord talked to say, blind Bartimaeus. She was able to visualise that street scene in Jericho very clearly and even to imagine being caught in the dust and the smells as the crowd came gathering around Jesus. She imagined Jesus asking Bartimaeus 'what would you have me to do for you?'. Sr Marie had suggested that at this point she might imagine Jesus then turning to her and asking her what she would have him do for *her*?

What did she really want from Jesus? Why had she come on this retreat? What was she seeking in her life? She felt that her life was drifting by, the children were growing up, her role was changing – what did she want to do with her future?

At the end it seemed not to matter that she had reached no momentous decisions during her week, what mattered was that she came away from it feeling refreshed and stimulated and ready to witness to her new and profound knowledge that she was loved by God. Instead of her middle life being a time of crisis she began to see that all kinds of new possibilities were opening up for her, in terms of prayer, self development, artistic discoveries and mission.

Individually guided retreats are held in many retreat centres, both Anglican and Roman Catholic, in different parts of the country. They are often held at times when people can take longer breaks, in the summer months and early in the year. Eight days goes very quickly and is worth attempting, though sometimes it is possible to go for a shorter time. However, on shorter stays people are sometimes frustrated to find that they are just beginning to settle into the retreat when it is time to stop.

There are also retreat houses run by religious orders who follow the Ignatian pattern of life. In these houses it is often possible to make your retreat at times other than those advertised. It is, however, helpful to be alongside a group of other people who are also in retreat. They help to keep you at it!

## ■ THEME RETREATS

This is, perhaps, one of the most modern retreat styles and has grown up rather in the way that creative holidays have come to be. People have gifts and talents they love to use – and how much we discover when we 'play'! A theme retreat combines some kind of artistic expression with times of quiet and prayer, as well as times of sharing. It is one that appeals to people of all ages, and you don't have to have a great talent to enjoy painting, calligraphy, embroidery, or whatever it is.

Gordon is now in his mid thirties, and he came to Christian faith while he was at college. It had happened that there was a group of Christians in his year with whom he became friendly. He enjoyed walking as a pastime and they invited him to join them on a pilgrimage to Taizé during the summer holidays. They hitched and walked through France and when they arrived at Taizé they found themselves in a very lively setting, with literally thousands of young people of many nationalities, although what seemed to draw people most was the silence in the community church. From the outside it looked like an aircraft hanger, but inside it was cool, quiet and welcoming. There were always people there praying together or making soft music. Several times a day the brothers came in and led prayers and singing. Organised seating had been abandoned and the (mostly young) people sat on the floor, more people in a church than Gordon had ever seen before.

Gordon was struck by the sense of community he experienced. There were meetings arranged for discussion between young people of other nationalities and other traditions, many of them from the former communist block, as well as from Africa, India and 'down under'.

Coming back to college after that summer was quite a bereavement, Gordon had felt part of something deep and important. He had also found a great deal of help in the silence and hoped that he would be able to return. Somehow it never happened.

Some years later one of his friends suggested a retreat, but the information he received sounded rather 'advanced' for him. He had appreciated the Taizé silence and found he could pray there, but he didn't think he could manage a whole weekend in silence! He decided that he would join a prayer and painting retreat the following summer. He found there was a group going to Normandy. Gordon was not an artist but had the feeling that he would discover something if he tried to paint. He was relieved to find that no one was expected to have previous experience or expertise.

The trip was half holiday, half retreat and turned out to be just what he wanted. In the group of 25 there was a tutor and a chaplain. They stayed in the guest house of a Benedictine abbey where they were given simple but delicious food and wine to go with it. Each night they said compline together and kept silence overnight. After breakfast there was a short prayer time, usually a meditation led by the chaplain, and then the group dispersed around the grounds and beyond with their painting things.

Both the tutor and the chaplain came round to them as they painted to see if they needed any help. Gordon had not painted since school but found it fascinating to try. He learned to look at things more carefully and to appreciate design and form. He spent time studying the abbey building and reflecting on how it was built to speak to those outside of the life within it. He noticed how the church stood above the other buildings, reaching up to God; how the gardens were laid out and how they supplied food for the community, and so on. He began to consider what his home said about him and his life, to wonder how he reflected his inner convictions and beliefs to the outside world.

At the end of each day and before supper the group gathered for the Eucharist, to give thanks for all that had been given to them that day. Each person then had a chance to show their day's painting and to talk about anything important that had occurred to them as they had worked. Every piece of work was valued for its meaning, not always its quality! This was a very important time to gather together the day's experiences and Gordon found the group both supportive and stimulating. He found he had more talent than he expected, but also realised that it was the experience of painting, not the end product, that was important.

In the evening they organised various activities: sometimes there was some input from the chaplain or the tutor, and sometimes they all sat round and talked and enjoyed the summer evenings – the more so for having discovered new ways of looking at things and becoming more alive to the world around them.

At the end of the week it was quite hard to break away from the group. Many others felt the same and so it was decided to have a day's reunion later in the autumn. They were amazed to realise how much and how deeply they had shared and how well they had got to know one another during the retreat. The focus on the presence of God in nature and the realisation of his presence among them, both while they prayed and while they painted, helped Gordon to go back and notice and appreciate God's presence even in the less beautiful setting of his home town. He had become part of a Christian community and looked forward to meeting up with them again.

## ■ PRIVATE RETREATS

There are some retreat houses that are only large enough to take a small number of guests. They are often attached to convents or monasteries and they welcome guests for short stays, usually up to a week. Diana went to stay with a small community of nuns in Kent for the inside of a week.

She had made retreats several times before and had always appreciated having some 'input' as well as times of quiet. This time she felt that she just wanted a retreat to think things through on her own. She used a pattern that was familiar to her and also decided to attend some of the services at the convent. She had taken the biography of a well known missionary doctor with her, and read that over meals which she had on her own. She was very tired and enjoyed having a rest in the afternoons before she went out for a walk. On her walks she often stopped to pick blackberries which she ate with her supper.

At the end, thinking back over some of the other retreats she had attended, she remembered they had been quite hard work and yet refreshing and stimulating. This time had been altogether quieter. No great insights had come, no high moments of discovery, but she felt when she got home that she had spent a quiet weekend with an old and trusted friend. She had returned to a loved and familiar place and found a welcome there.

## ■ AWARENESS WORKSHOPS

These are not strictly retreats because they have a different focus. While the workshops are not directly concerned with helping people in their relationship with God, this is likely to be a spin-off when they find a better relationship with themselves. The focus is self-discovery as a means to discovering the God who made us in his image. Many people are hampered by a poor self-image and the workshop will help them to a healthier acceptance of their giftedness.

## ■ THE MYERS BRIGGS WORKSHOP

This is based on the psychologist Carl Jung's theory of personality type. It helps people to recognise their own gifts, and the gifts of others. Although we appear to differ in a fairly random way, Jung suggested that there are some basic patterns to which we are drawn because of certain preferences inherent in our natures. Preferences for the outer world of action or the inner world of ideas; preference for taking in information through the physical senses or via our intuition; preference for processing the information by logical thought or through our value system, and so on. Recognising the effect of these preferences helps us to use them freely and prevents many misunderstandings.

It is not a method of dividing people into boxes, but of helping them to appreciate and understand themselves – and others. The fact that you are an extrovert and I am an introvert means that you have a preference for functioning in the outer world of action, while my preference is for functioning in the inner world of ideas and imagination. You will positively gain energy from being with other people, and will enjoy relaxing in their company. My energy will be sapped by being with a crowd and this means that when I take time off I shall look for somewhere quiet to curl up with a book, while you will want to be sociable.

Another example might be about the approach to prayer – a person who has a preference for using their logical thinking function will see prayer as a search for truth; the person who is primarily fired by their value system will seek prayer as a place of harmony and peace.

You may begin to see that there is no right or wrong about it, but a recognition of what is going on very quickly irons out many problems, allowing people to feel affirmed in their own viewpoint and tolerant towards others. An understanding of the different ways in which people approach things helps people to work together in a more constructive way, so a workshop can be valuable in enabling teamwork. A recognition that my weakness may be your strength, and your weakness my strength, can be threatening – or it can be liberating and open the way for cooperation and mutual satisfaction. We need each other.

# ■ THE ENNEAGRAM WORKSHOP

This is another workshop about personality type (ennea means nine, and there are nine types in this schema). It is based in ancient wisdom, most of which has been handed down by oral tradition, and about which little had been written until the last decade or so.

The enneagram is another tool which may help people to self-understanding and self-acceptance. It offers some pointers to the path we may take if we are to grow and develop spiritually and psychologically. It helps us to understand what happens if, say under stress, we regress. The types are related in a particular way and portrayed as nine points on the circumference of a circle. Our type, according the enneagram, is not fixed, we constantly move between our dark side and our potential. Our dark side (our compulsions) and our potential (our redeemed selves) pull us back or lead us forward respectively. People of the same type are likely to find things in common as they discover their strengths and as they struggle to overcome difficulties and blind spots. The enneagram will bring out the positive strengths of each type and indicate the direction in which you may need to move in order to become a more mature, more authentic person.

The basic workshop takes two to four days. If

you find this helpful you may have the opportunity of going on a retreat which is based on the discoveries made in the workshop. This would provide an opportunity for developing some of the paths that are suggested for greater self- understanding, as well as processing some of the muddles and failings of the past.

## ■ JOURNALLING WORKSHOPS

Journalling helps us to reflect on our lives. Many of us cannot see how God has been active in our lives and this is often because we do not take time to reflect on what has happened to us. When we do we often find some unexpected treasures. Sometimes, too, there is some hurt in past relationships and experiences that we have good reason to block out. If this has been your misfortune it would be wise to tell the leader at the beginning, so that she or he can be sensitive to your difficulties.

At the workshop people are helped to spend time remembering and recording important relationships and events in their lives. One exercise could be to consider what might have happened if a different choice had been made at one of life's crossroads. Is there something to be learned from it? Working towards the big decisions in our lives is something for which we need discernment, we need to draw on past experience and gain as much insight and information as possible.

Unfinished business from past relationships may be healed, developed or understood when there is time and some guidance in the way we look at them. Unsatisfactory relationships that have left pain, anger or fear may be helped towards resolution.

Patterns of behaviour are particular to each of us, sometimes they are not altogether in our control and can be quite destructive. Thinking about these patterns, writing them down and reflecting on them may enable us to see how they form, for good or ill, and how we may make more conscious choices about the way our lives should go in future.

People attending a journalling workshop are encouraged to go on working with their journal, making notes of important or significant events, feelings, relationships or insights. Writing things down helps us to process what happens in our lives, leaving us freer to move on without fear of losing touch with our important experiences.

Many people find it valuable to keep a prayer diary. Making a record of a time of prayer helps to establish in us a habit of reflection   we look back over the time and notice where our attention was focused and how we experienced

God. Our entry may also include a reflection over the day to see how prayer and life have been linked.

Keeping a record over weeks and months will enable us to look back and see a broader view of the way that God moves in our lives. We shall make connections between things that we might otherwise have forgotten as we read through our experiences again. A prayer diary is especially useful if we sometimes talk to a friend or guide, because we shall have important material at our fingertips.

## ■ RETREATS IN DAILY LIFE

This may sound like a contradiction in terms, but many people have real difficulty in getting away from home even for a weekend, whether it is because of the family or the finances. Retreat houses try to keep their prices down as much as possible and by commercial standards they are amazingly low, but it is still too much for many people even to consider.

Need creates new ideas and there are now a number of different retreat styles that are given on a non-residential basis. This is a different kind of retreat and there are things that you miss out on – like keeping silence with a group of others – but you can still spend quality time with God by making a retreat in daily life.

You may find such a retreat through your church or your parish. There are several possibilities:

- The Open Door Retreat, nine weeks.
- A Way of Life, a 14-week programme, meeting once a week.
- Retreats in the Parish, usually every night for one week
- The Spiritual Exercises of St Ignatius, which an individual can make in daily life over a number of months

Of course you are not expected to keep silence for the duration of these retreats! What is expected is that you should spend a certain amount of time in prayer each day as well as some time reflecting on how your everyday activities and relationships interact with your prayers. It helps to bring life and prayer together. If you decide to join an Open Door or A Way of Life retreat, you should feel comfortable about sharing some of your experience with others in the group.

Everyone goes at their own pace, most will make notes about their experience during the week to help them reflect as well as remember. There is usually more than one leader, but each retreatant will have someone they can refer to if they need to.

This kind of retreat is becoming more and more popular because it is so flexible and can be used with groups of people to suit their lifestyles. There can be retreats for young mums in the mornings or for OAPs in the afternoons. Trust and support grow visibly within the group.

No doubt the future will bring new forms of retreats which will arise from the needs of the moment. God is a God who moves us on and invites us to go with him. If we have found a quiet place within we shall be ready to go out and greet all as our neighbours in Christ. For we go 'inwards' in order to be strengthened to go out to others with the love of God flowing more freely through us.

**For you to do:** Stop for a moment and recall the different kinds of retreats described. Which come first to your mind as the ones you feel drawn to? Perhaps it is just one.

Go back and read that section or those sections again.

# 7

# MOVING ON

BEFORE PUTTING this book away write for details about retreats being held in the current year. *The Vision* is available from the National Retreat Association, Liddon House, 24 South Audley Street, London W1Y 5DL. Tel 071-493 3534. It costs £2.50 plus 70p postage (1994).

You might like to become a member of one or other of the denominational retreat groups. Quite recently, groups that have formed within the Anglican, Roman Catholic, Methodist, Baptist, United Reformed and Quaker traditions, joined forces to become the National Retreat Association. Membership entitles you to a copy of *The Vision* each year and it also helps the association to spread and promote retreats. Spending time with God is a vital part of our Christian witness, and what better way is there of renewing our vision and our energy? It would be good if this way could be more widely known.

The National Retreat Association produces separate leaflets about the different types of retreats and workshops. They may be able to link you up with someone who can give you more local information, and they also have information about people who are available to lead different types of retreats and some of the workshops mentioned.

The association may also be able to advise you of someone to contact if you need encouragement and help to follow up your retreat experience. It isn't always easy to know where to go when you come down from the mountain. Perhaps you know where to ask for help and guidance, if not the NRA may be able to help.

At the end of a retreat it is quite usual to experience a bit of a 'high' and then to feel an anti-climax. If you have been dealing with an important agenda and been stimulated and excited about your new discoveries it is inevitable that you will notice some sense of loss afterwards. Do not worry, God has not gone away; just thank him for giving you a glimpse of his love in the days before. He has promised to be with you always and he is faithful to his promises.